Grace, Please

AN EASY-TO-FOLLOW, DAILY GUIDE FOR CHANGING YOUR LIFE THROUGH THE POWER OF THE ROSARY

Piper Scheck

Grace, Please

ISBN: 1515260720
ISBN-13: 978-1515260721

Printed in the United States of America.

Second Edition

To Him, Through Her

Contents:

A special thank you to The Rosary Center, run by the Dominican Fathers in Portland, OR (Rosary-Center.org), for enthusiastically sharing their work in order to propagate the Rosary in every way possible.

Also thank you, Glo, for so lovingly describing the detail and depth of your ongoing relationship with Our Blessed Mother, and for introducing us to Her.

.

Introduction

Hi there.

Let me start off by introducing myself, and telling you what I am not. I am not a nun. I am not a Catholic-school graduate. I'm not a church worker or religious writer or even someone who regularly contributes spiritually-minded comments on blogs.

What I am is a wife, mother and generally-regular person who stumbled, what I thought was by accident, into a wealth of inspiring information about what the Rosary is, how to pray it, and why people do it. That information motivated me into praying the Rosary regularly. And then my life didn't change on the outside that much, but in my heart, *everything* changed. And that's the extent of my professional Rosary training.

As you can see, I couldn't be farther from being an expert on the Rosary. Which is actually my point!

Anyone can pray and receive the life-changing graces of the Rosary. You don't have to have excessive time on your hands. You don't have to be a sweet old lady or a saint. You don't even have to be Catholic! All you have to be is one of God's children, and well, I hate to point out the obvious on that one but...yes, YOU qualify!

What is the Rosary?

The Rosary is a set of prayers that are said while reflecting on a total of 20 Mysteries, or stories, about the life of Jesus and His mother, Mary. The word "rosary" comes from the Latin word *rosarium*, or, "rose garden". The rose is often associated with Mary, and saying this set of prayers has been compared to offering a bouquet of roses to Our Holy Mother.

The Rosary is often misunderstood to simply be the repetition of the same set of prayers over and over. The true essence of the Rosary lies in your mediation and reflection on the stories about the life of Christ as you're saying the prayers. As Father Ronan Murphy put it, the Rosary is "...the Bible on a string".

Most of the prayers of the Rosary are directed to Mary in the form of the "Hail Mary" prayer, which asks the Blessed Mother to pray to Her Son on our behalf.

Mary is a deeply merciful and compassionate mother; she hears all of our pleas and takes every single one to Jesus. No matter who we are. No matter where we are in our life or our faith. No matter what we've done, or said, or thought, or not done or not said or not thought, etc., etc.

Mary, like Her Son, deeply loves every one of us and calls us to a deeper relationship with her and Jesus. Praying the Rosary is a direct route to strengthening those relationships and receiving the magnificent blessings that come with growing closer to Our Lord and His Blessed Mother.

Saint Louis de Montfort, a French priest at the end of the 17th century, devoted himself to Mary as a spiritual pathway to Jesus through His Mother, a concept summarized by the phrase "To Jesus, through Mary". Within that concept, praying the Rosary is actually praying to God, through the Blessed Mother herself. What better way to approach Our Lord than through the Mother that He adores so much?

Each decade (or, announcement of the Mystery, set of one "Our Father", ten "Hail Mary"s and one "Glory Be" prayers) of the Rosary represents one Mystery. One complete set of rosary beads generally represents five decades, or, five Mysteries outlining the events in the life of Christ. (For my fellow visual learners, there's a "Rosary Beads Guide" near the end of the book).

Each set of five Mysteries (or, one set of rosary beads) is arranged into a theme of biblical events. There are four themes:

1. The **JOYFUL** Mysteries (stories around Jesus' birth and young life)

2. The **LUMINOUS** Mysteries (stories around Jesus' life as an adult)

3. The **SORROWFUL** Mysteries (stories around Jesus' last days / the Crucifixion)

4. The **GLORIOUS** Mysteries (stories around Jesus' Resurrection and Ascension)

The themes are assigned to different days of the week:

Monday:	**JOYFUL** Mysteries
Tuesday:	**SORROWFUL** Mysteries
Wednesday:	**GLORIOUS** Mysteries
Thursday:	**LUMINOUS** Mysteries
Friday:	**SORROWFUL** Mysteries
Saturday:	**JOYFUL** Mysteries
Sunday:	**GLORIOUS** Mysteries (except Sundays in Lent = **SORROWFUL** Mysteries and Sundays in Advent = **JOYFUL**)

The History of the Rosary

Though there are different versions of the origin of the Rosary, a commonly held belief is that in 1214 the Virgin Mary revealed the Rosary to St. Dominic in an apparition. St. Dominic de Guzman was a Spanish priest who went on to found the Dominican Order of the Roman Catholic church. The Dominican Order of Priests in Portland, OR runs the Rosary Center (Rosary-Center.org), which provided a good bit of information that appears in this book. So, in theory, much of what you have in your hands can be traced right back to Mary!

Around two centuries after St. Dominic's lifetime, a Dominican Father named Alanus de la Roche ("Blessed Alan") became a strong advocate and promoter of the Rosary. Pious tradition states that Mary appeared to Blessed Alan, and shared with him 15 amazing promises of special graces and protection for all people who regularly pray the Rosary. (It is also said that Mary shared these promises with St. Dominic in an apparition, around 200 years earlier). Mary's beautiful 15 Promises are listed in the next section of this book.

Throughout history many people have lauded the power of praying the Rosary:

"Give me an army saying the Rosary and I will conquer the world."

- **Blessed Pope Pius IX**

"There is no problem, I tell you, no matter how difficult it is, that we cannot resolve by the prayer of the Holy Rosary."

- **Sister Lucia dos Santos, Fatima Seer**

"The greatest method of praying is to pray the Rosary."

- **Saint Francis de Sales**

"You shall obtain all you ask of me by the recitation of the Rosary."

- **Our Lady to Blessed Alan de la Roche**

"The Rosary is the most beautiful and the most rich in graces of all prayers"

- **Pope Saint Pius X**

"If you greet her, she will answer you right away and converse with you!"

- **St. Bernardine of Siena**

"I recite the 15 Mysteries of the Rosary every day."

- **Pope Francis**

How to Physically Pray the Rosary

The Rosary can be said by using a set of rosary beads to mark your place as you pray, or it can be said by simply using your fingers. You can say the Rosary out loud, or you can say it in your head. You can say it with someone else, including with a group at your church, or you can say it alone. You can turn down your radio and say it in the car.

You can even pull it up on YouTube and pick your favorite version of someone else saying it, and follow along via your ear buds.

You can break the decades of the Rosary up and say them at different times during the day. You can say them while you're running or walking or vacuuming. Even if you accidentally fall asleep while saying them at night, rumor has it that angels will finish them for you.

The "how" pales in comparison to the "what", which is the fact that you're regularly offering up your time to think and pray and reflect on the life of Jesus while considering the implications of His teachings on your own life. And this is the very act that opens you up to receiving the graces that Mary and Jesus want so much to give to you!

Just like every other good habit you've ever picked up, you will get better at saying the Rosary with time. That might sound funny, but as the words to the prayers and the Mysteries come to you more naturally, it will become easier for you to enter into a meditative state where you'll feel more directly connected to Jesus and Mary in your conversation. And yes, it really is *that* awesome.

Now, not to be bossy, but when you first start saying the

Rosary, you may want to consider reading through every bullet of each Mystery. You are essentially teaching yourself the stories, then training your brain to apply them to your own life with the reflection point at the end.

As you pray the Rosary more and more, soon the entire story and reflection point will come to mind at just the mention of the Mystery name. At this point you can get really fancy and start inserting your own reflection points and customized prayers for each Mystery. And this is when that connectedness to Our Mother and Lord really takes off. It happens faster than you'd think.

Special Intentions: Before or after you say each decade is a great time to offer up special intentions that are on your heart or prayers for others in need.

- Some people say each decade in honor of a family member.
- Some pray for the lonely, sick and suffering.
- Some pray for the repose of the souls of loved ones (by name) who have gone before them.
- Some pray for those who have passed that have no one else to pray for them.
- Some pray for those in Purgatory.
- Some pray for peace.
- Some pray for the intentions of our priests, nuns, bishops and the pope.
- Some offer the intention to whomever Mary deems needs it the most, whether you personally know that person or not.

Remembering someone in your Rosary is the ultimate gift! It is powerful and it is free!

A Note to Groups: If you do end up saying the Rosary with someone else or in a group, traditionally one person will announce each Mystery and then lead each prayer. The bolded sections of the prayers indicate where the group chimes in together to finish the prayer the leader started.

The bolded sections of the Mysteries are abridged "highlights", which group leaders may want to read (as opposed to reading all of the bullets in the Mystery) in the interest of time.

Benefits: Spiritual and Otherwise

Aside from prayer being scientifically proven to reduce anxiety and depression as well as to improve optimism, this particular form of prayerful mediation has been known to result in wonderful, miraculous things happening to those who pray this way. I'm being vague here for a reason. You have your own, unique path to the Blessed Mother! Yours is different than mine! You're entitled to your own, unique Google-binge so you can read the amazing stories people accredit to their praying the Rosary, yourself!

Though, a friendly note of warning: I spent three nights straight finding and reading these stories online. You may want to wrap up your "day job" responsibilities before you query anything.

Ok, I can't stand it. Here are some cheater search terms: "Battle of Lepanto" or "8 Jesuit Priests Survive Hiroshima Bomb" or "Austria Rosary 1955". AMAZE-ing.

Say, while you're at your keyboard, maybe shoot an email to that one friend or great-uncle that you know prays the Rosary regularly? See if they have any stories for you. (This is a set-up. I know they do.)

And then whenever you step away from the computer and begin to pray the Rosary, here's a pleasant by-product you may notice: Just as spending time with a new friend allows you to get to know him or her better, spending time thinking about the lives of Jesus and Mary allows you to feel as if you know them better, too- immediately. This feels *real* good.

And then when you hit your Rosary stride and start to pray it pretty regularly, you will likely notice that even though you're reflecting on the same 20 stories over and over, because they are biblical, (AKA the *Living Word*), they seem to always have a new relevance to you. As life throws you curve balls, you often get your answer during your Rosary, sometimes from a story you've heard a gazillion times. It's spooky great.

You may also find that the stories become part of your decision-making toolset, and you may catch yourself considering how Jesus and Mary handled a certain situation in their lives when facing new or recurring challenges in your own life. All of a sudden old problems have new solutions. See how this works? The Rosary can even infiltrate your decision making! Spiritual guidance while figuring out problems! Heavenly good ideas! Enlightened day-to-day input! Where is the downside, here?

Oh, and wait until you see the 15 Promises Mary makes to those who regularly pray the Rosary! Just reading through them gives instant stress-relief. As a former semi-professional Debbie Downer, I can tell you that knowing Mary's Promises and regularly praying the Rosary has had a quantifiable impact on my daily anxiety level. As in, my vitals are different. I literally sleep better. I enjoy our kids' sports instead of planning the route for the paramedics. But enough about me...Your path. Your path.

Well, actually back to me. I have one more thing I want to share with you, and then I'll pull it back to you at the end of the next paragraph, I promise! Here's the Rosary mantra, main point, tagline if you will that changed not only my heart but also my mind:

He's got this. She's got this.

After realizing through prayer that these two statements have consistently been true in my life and I trust will continue to be true, I was able to loosen my white-knuckle grasp on the world and all of the goings-on in it, and am now thoroughly enjoying our many blessings so much more than I did before. That was *my* thing...you'll hear your own mantra and have your own life-changing realization specific to whatever is preventing joy and peace in *your* life. You may not know what it is yet, but Mary does. So does Jesus. All you have to do is pray, listen, repeat. Keep asking...they will answer.

For the Planners...

One Rosary (5 decades) usually takes around 25 minutes to pray. While you're learning it, plan on about 30. Rosary groups usually take about 25-30 minutes, too.

So now that you've got the basics of how to pray the Rosary and we've established that it doesn't really even take very long, how's about giving it a go? Why not see for yourself what happens to you when you pray the Rosary?

I actually have some idea of how this is going to go for you, which is why I've include a little "Notes" section at the end of the book, anticipating that you will indeed need it. I'm excited for you. You're in good hands – the best, actually.

And when you're done with this copy of your book, please be sure to pass it along to someone else who could use it! Proverbial five bucks says you'll have that someone in mind by the time you finish your first decade.

Good luck to you and God Bless you!

Mary's
15 Promises

AS REVEALED TO ST. DOMINIC AND BLESSED ALAN

©Boris15 | Dreamstime.com

PROMISE 1:

To all those who shall recite my Rosary devoutly, I promise my special protection and very great graces.

PROMISE 2:

Those who shall persevere in the recitation of my Rosary shall receive some signal grace.

PROMISE 3:

The Rosary shall be a very
powerful armor against hell; it
will destroy vice, deliver from sin,
and dispel heresy.

PROMISE 4:

The Rosary will make virtue and good works flourish, and will obtain for souls the most abundant divine mercies; it will substitute in the hearts love of God for love of the world, and will lift them to the desire of heavenly and eternal things. How many souls shall sanctify themselves by this means!

PROMISE 5:

Those who trust themselves to me through the Rosary shall not perish.

PROMISE 6:

Those who shall recite my Rosary devoutly, meditating on its mysteries, shall not be overwhelmed by misfortune. The sinner shall be converted; the just shall grow in grace and become worthy of eternal life.

PROMISE 7:

Those truly devoted to my Rosary

shall not die without the

Sacraments of the Church.

PROMISE 8:

Those who recite my Rosary shall
find during their life and at their
death the light of God, the
fullness of His Graces, and shall
share in the merits of the blessed.

PROMISE 9:

I shall deliver very promptly from Purgatory the souls devoted to my Rosary.

PROMISE 10:

The true children of my Rosary

shall enjoy great glory in Heaven.

PROMISE 11:

What you ask through my Rosary,

you shall obtain.

PROMISE 12:

Those who propagate my Rosary

shall be aided by me in all their

necessities.

PROMISE 13:

I have obtained from my Son
that all the members of the
Rosary Confraternity shall have
for their brethren the saints of
heaven during their life and at
the hour of death.

PROMISE 14:

Those who recite my Rosary

faithfully are all my beloved

children, the brothers and sisters

of Jesus Christ.

PROMISE 15:

Devotion to my Rosary is a great sign of predestination.

LEGEND

Our Father

Our Father, Who art in Heaven, hallowed be Thy name. Thy kingdom come, Thy Will be done, on earth as it is in Heaven. **Give us this day our daily bread, and forgive us our trespasses as we forgive those who trespass against us. Lead us not into temptation, but deliver us from evil. Amen.**

Hail Mary

Hail Mary, full of grace, the Lord is with thee. Blesssed are thou among women, and blessed is the fruit of thy womb, Jesus. **Holy Mary, Mother of God, pray for us sinners, now and at the hour of our death. Amen.**

Glory Be

Glory be to the Father, and to the Son, and to the Holy Spirit. **As it was in the beginning, is now, and ever shall be, world without end. Amen.**

* If saying the Rosary with a group, the leader recites the un-bolded sections of the prayers alone, then the group joins in and says the bolded sections together.

Monday

THE JOYFUL MYSTERIES

©Benjamin Vess | Dreamstime.com

MONDAY

The Joyful Mysteries

Make the
SIGN
of the
CROSS

Say the **Apostles Creed**:

I believe in God, the Father Almighty, Creator of Heaven and earth; and in Jesus Christ, His only Son, our Lord: Who was conceived by the Holy Spirit, born of the Virgin Mary; suffered under Pontius Pilate, was crucified, died and was buried. He descended into hell; the third day He rose again from the dead; He ascended into Heaven, is seated at the right hand of God the Father Almighty; from thence He shall come to judge the living and the dead. **I believe in the Holy Spirit, the Holy Catholic Church, the communion of Saints, the forgiveness of sins, the resurrection of the body, and life everlasting. Amen.**

(Groups may wish to read the abridged, **bolded** sections of the Mystery only)

MONDAY

The Joyful Mysteries

The First Mystery: The Annunciation

Portions paraphrased from Luke 1: 26-38 NAB

- God prepared Mary from her conception to be the Mother of Jesus, free from original sin.

- **The Angel Gabriel appears to Mary and greets her.**

- **Mary is frightened and confused.**

- Gabriel assures her: "Do not be afraid, Mary, for you have found favor with God."

- **He says: "Behold, you will conceive in your womb and bear a son, and you shall name him Jesus."**

- **Mary is worried because she's pledged to be married to Joseph, and has made a vow of virginity.**

- During this time in history, a woman could be stoned to death for becoming pregnant out of wedlock.

- **Mary considers all of this and bravely answers: "Behold, I am the handmaid of the Lord. May it be it done unto me according to your word."**

- Dear God, what are You asking of me today? How will I answer You?

Spiritual Fruit : Humility

Oh my Jesus, forgive us our sins. Save us from the fires of hell. Lead all souls to Heaven, especially those in most need of Thy Mercy. Amen.

MONDAY

 2nd Mystery

The Joyful Mysteries

The Second Mystery: The Visitation

Portions paraphrased from Luke 1:39-45 NAB

- Mary's cousin, Elizabeth, had become pregnant, despite her age and many years of infertility.

- When Mary hears the news, she plans to visit Elizabeth, even though they live 80 miles apart and Mary is newly pregnant herself.

- The journey is long and difficult, but Mary is joyful because she knows she's carrying the Son of God.

- When Mary arrives, Elizabeth's baby jumps in her womb at the sound of Mary's voice.

- Elizabeth says, "And how does this happen to me, that the mother of my Lord should come to me?"

- Mary replies, "My soul proclaims the greatness of the Lord and my spirit rejoices in God my savior."

- Mary stays with Elizabeth and helps her for the next three months until the birth of John the Baptist.

- Holy Spirit, please lead me to whomever is in need of my help today. Help me to know how I can best serve him or her.

Spiritual Fruit : Love of Neighbor

Oh my Jesus, forgive us our sins. Save us from the fires of hell. Lead all souls to Heaven, especially those in most need of Thy Mercy. Amen.

MONDAY

The Joyful Mysteries

The Third Mystery: The Nativity

Portions paraphrased from Luke 2:1-20 NAB

- Caesar Augustus required that everyone in the Roman domain register for the census in their native town.

- Joseph's family was from Bethlehem, so he and Mary travel from Nazareth to Bethlehem to register.

- **When they arrive in Bethlehem, Mary goes into labor, and she and Joseph try to find a room at the inn.**

- **There's no room for them there, so Mary gives birth to Her Son in a cave, wraps Him in cloths, and lays Him in a manger.**

- **Jesus is born into poverty to teach detachment from earthly things.**

- **Mary, still a Virgin, is utterly joyful as she cradles her Son.**

- **An angel appears to shepherds nearby and says, "...today in the city of David a Savior has been born for you who is Messiah and Lord."**

- What earthly/ material things are hindering my relationship with God? Lord, please help me let go of any things that are keeping me from becoming closer to You.

Spiritual Fruit : Poverty of Spirit

Oh my Jesus, forgive us our sins. Save us from the fires of hell. Lead all souls to Heaven, especially those in most need of Thy Mercy. Amen.

MONDAY

4th
Mystery

The Joyful Mysteries

The Fourth Mystery: The Presentation

Portions paraphrased from Luke 2:22-40 NAB

- The Law of Moses required that every family consecrate (or, "dedicate") their firstborn son to the Lord.

- **Mary and Joseph bring Jesus to the temple for His consecration.**

- Simeon was a "righteous and devout" man who had been told by the Holy Spirit that he would see the Messiah before he died.

- **When the Holy Family enters the temple, Simeon immediately recognizes Jesus.**

- **Simeon takes Jesus into his arms and says, "Now, Master, you may let your servant go in peace, according to your word, for mine eyes have seen your salvation..."**

- Mary and Joseph are amazed at what Simeon says about Jesus.

- **Simeon tells Mary, "Behold, this child is destined for the fall and rise of many in Israel, and to be a sign that will be contradicted (and you yourself a sword will pierce)..."**

- Even Mary, the Mother of God, didn't know God's plan for her all at once; it was revealed to her little by little. Mary, help me to be patient as I learn God's plan for me.

Spiritual Fruit : Purity of Mind and Body

Oh my Jesus, forgive us our sins. Save us from the fires of hell. Lead all souls to Heaven, especially those in most need of Thy Mercy. Amen.

Christ and the Pharisees Alexander Bida 1874 (PD-1923 Wikimedia.org)

MONDAY

5th Mystery

The Joyful Mysteries

The Fifth Mystery: The Finding of Jesus in the Temple

Portions paraphrased from Luke 2:41-52 NAB

- **When Jesus is twelve years old, Mary and Joseph take Him with them to the festival of the Passover.**

- **When the festival is over, Mary and Joseph set off for home, unknowingly without Jesus.**

- Once Mary and Joseph realize Jesus is missing, they start frantically searching for Him.

- **After three days of searching, they find Jesus in the temple in Jerusalem, talking with the teachers and doctors.**

- Everyone listening to Jesus is amazed by His knowledge and perspective.

- **When Mary tells Jesus she and Joseph were anxiously looking for Him, Jesus says, "Why were you looking for Me? Did you not know that I must be in my Father's house?"**

- **Jesus goes home with Mary and Joseph and is obedient to them.**

- Dear Lord, help me to be obedient to what You want of me as opposed to what the world wants of me.

Spiritual Fruit : Obedience

Our Father · Hail Mary · Hail Mary · Hail Mary · Hail Mary · Hail Mary · Hail Mary · Hail Mary · Hail Mary · Hail Mary · Hail Mary · GLORY BE

Oh my Jesus, forgive us our sins. Save us from the fires of hell. Lead all souls to Heaven, especially those in most need of Thy Mercy. Amen.

MONDAY

The Joyful Mysteries

Hail, Holy Queen,

Mother of Mercy, our life, our sweetness, and our hope! To thee do we cry, poor, banished children of Eve; to thee do we send up our sighs, mourning and weeping in this valley of tears. Turn then, most gracious advocate, thine eyes of mercy toward us, and after this our exile, show unto us the blessed fruit of thy womb, Jesus. Oh clement, oh loving, oh sweet Virgin Mary! Pray for us, oh Holy Mother of God, that we may be made worthy of the promises of Christ. Amen.

Let us pray, oh God, Whose only begotten Son, by His life, death, and resurrection, has purchased for us the rewards of eternal life, grant, we beseech Thee, that by meditating upon these mysteries of the Most Holy Rosary of the Blessed Virgin Mary, that we may imitate what they contain and obtain what they promise, through the same Christ Our Lord. Amen.

Tuesday

THE SORROWFUL MYSTERIES

TUESDAY
The Sorrowful Mysteries

Make the
SIGN
of the
CROSS

Say the **Apostles Creed**

I believe in God, the Father Almighty, Creator of
Heaven and earth; and in Jesus Christ, His only Son,
our Lord: Who was conceived by the Holy Spirit, born
of the Virgin Mary; suffered under Pontius Pilate, was
crucified, died and was buried. He descended into
hell; the third day He rose again from the dead; He
ascended into Heaven, is seated at the right hand of
God the Father Almighty; from thence He shall come
to judge the living and the dead. **I believe in the Holy
Spirit, the Holy Catholic Church, the communion of
Saints, the forgiveness of sins, the resurrection of the
body, and life everlasting. Amen.**

The Garden of Gethsemane | Pixabay.com

TUESDAY

1st Mystery

The Sorrowful Mysteries

The First Mystery: The Agony in the Garden

Portions paraphrased from Luke 22:39-46 and Matthew 26:36-46 NAB

- **Jesus and his disciples went to a place called Gethsemane to pray.**

- **Jesus tells Peter, James and John that His soul is, "overwhelmed with sorrow to the point of death."**

- **He walks a short distance away from them and prays, "Father, if you are willing, take this cup away from me; still, not my will but yours be done."**

- **Here Jesus foresees the sins of all mankind, and is so overcome with anguish that His sweat becomes drops of blood.**

- An angel appears to Him to strengthen Him.

- **He returns to the sleeping disciples and says to Peter, "So you could not keep watch with me for one hour? Watch and pray that you may not undergo the test."**

- Just then a crowd approaches and Jesus is bound and led away.

- Jesus paid the ultimate price for God's Will to be done, so that we could live eternally. Have I taken the time today to remember how intensely Jesus loves me?

Spiritual Fruit : God's Will Be Done

Jesus at the Pillar, Unknown, Barcelona, Italy (Photo by Jose Luiz Bernardes Ribeiro 2014 CC-BY-SA-3.0 Wikimedia.org)

TUESDAY

The Sorrowful Mysteries

The Second Mystery: The Scourging at the Pillar

Portions paraphrased from Mark 15:15, John 19:1 and Isaiah 53:5 NAB

- Jesus is taken to the Jewish High Priest, where He is insulted and falsely accused.

- The Jewish leaders take Jesus to Pilate, since only he can order the death penalty.

- Pilate can "find no guilt in him", but to appease the Jews, he orders that Jesus be scourged.

- The Romans tie Jesus to a pillar and fiercely scourge Him with a short, whip-like weapon that has sharp bones or iron balls on the end of it.

- This painful scourging fulfills Isaiah's prophesy from the Old Testament, that Jesus would be "pierced for our sins" and "crushed for our iniquity".

- It's believed the Blessed Mother, Mary Magdalene and other apostles witnessed the scourging of Jesus.

- Oh Mary, how awful it must have been to see your Son suffer this way. Please help me be worthy of the pain He endured for me.

Spiritual Fruit : Mortification of the Senses

Oh my Jesus, forgive us our sins. Save us from the fires of hell. Lead all souls to Heaven, especially those in most need of Thy Mercy. Amen.

TUESDAY

The Sorrowful Mysteries

The Third Mystery: The Crowning with Thorns

Portions paraphrased from Matthew 27:11-29 and John 18:33-36 and 19:5 NAB

- **Pilate asks, "Are you the King of the Jews?" Jesus responds, "My kingdom does not belong to this world."**

- The Roman soldiers take Jesus into the praetorium (or "common hall") and gather all around Him.

- **The soldiers strip Jesus and put an old purple cloak on Him.**

- **They twist together a crown of thorns and push it into Jesus' head.**

- They put a staff in His right hand, spit on Him and mock Him for saying He is a king.

- **"Hail, king of the Jews!" they shout, and they take the staff from His hand and hit Him on the head with it several times.**

- They then strip the robe off Jesus' bloodied back and shoulders and put His original clothes back on.

- Jesus submitted to this terrible humiliation to atone for our pride.

- Lord, please help me to remember Your sacrifice in the praetorium so that I resist feelings of pride, indignation and entitlement.

Spiritual Fruit : Reign of Christ in Our Hearts

Oh my Jesus, forgive us our sins. Save us from the fires of hell. Lead all souls to Heaven, especially those in most need of Thy Mercy. Amen.

TUESDAY

4th Mystery

The Sorrowful Mysteries

The Fourth Mystery: The Carrying of the Cross

Paraphrased from Matthew 27:32-33, John 19:17, Luke 23:26-31 NAB, Stations of the Cross

- **Jesus is forced to carry His own cross to the place where he will be crucified, called Golgotha, or "Place of the Skull".**

- The cross is heavy, and Jesus is weakened from the scourging and lack of food, water and sleep.

- **Jesus falls under the weight of the cross three times.**

- **He sees His Mother in the crowd, and they exchange a poignant glance.**

- **Seeing that He's become too weak to continue on His own, the soldiers order Simon of Cyrene to help Jesus carry His cross.**

- A woman in the crowd named Veronica has deep pity for Jesus as He passes by, and she wipes His face with her veil.

- A miraculous impression of Jesus' face is left on the cloth.

- **Jesus says to the crying women who were following Him, "...do not weep for me; weep instead for yourselves and for your children."**

- Dear God, please help me to remember Your Son's excruciating walk when I face difficult challenges in my own life.

Spiritual Fruit : Patient Bearing of Trials

Oh my Jesus, forgive us our sins. Save us from the fires of hell. Lead all souls to Heaven, especially those in most need of Thy Mercy. Amen.

TUESDAY
The Sorrowful Mysteries

The Fifth Mystery: The Crucifixion

Portions paraphrased from Mark 15:21-41 and Luke 23:32-46 NAB

- **The soldiers bind and then nail Jesus' hands and feet to the cross.**

- **Jesus prays as he is being crucified, "Father, forgive them, they know not what they do."**

- One of the two criminals being crucified next to Jesus challenges Him, telling Jesus to save Himself and them if He's really the One.

- The other criminal humbly asks Jesus to remember him when He comes into His kingdom, and Jesus replies, "Amen, I say to you, today you will be with me in Paradise."

- **Around 3PM, Jesus cries out, "My God, my God, why have you forsaken me?"**

- **And then, in a loud voice, Jesus says, "Father, into your hands I commend my spirit," and he breathed his last breath and died.**

- **Jesus is taken down off the cross and laid in the arms of His Mother.**

- Jesus, You asked Our Father to forgive those who crucified You as you were dying on the cross. Please help me forgive any and all sins against me, easily and quickly, in Your Name.

Spiritual Fruit : Pardoning of Injuries

Oh my Jesus, forgive us our sins. Save us from the fires of hell. Lead all souls to Heaven, especially those in most need of Thy Mercy. Amen.

TUESDAY

The Sorrowful Mysteries

Hail, Holy Queen.

Mother of Mercy, our life, our sweetness, and our hope! To thee do we cry, poor, banished children of Eve; to thee do we send up our sighs, mourning and weeping in this valley of tears. Turn then, most gracious advocate, thine eyes of mercy toward us, and after this our exile, show unto us the blessed fruit of thy womb, Jesus. Oh clement, oh loving, oh sweet Virgin Mary! Pray for us, oh Holy Mother of God, that we may be made worthy of the promises of Christ. Amen.

Let us pray, oh God, Whose only begotten Son, by His life, death, and resurrection, has purchased for us the rewards of eternal life, grant, we beseech Thee, that by meditating upon these mysteries of the Most Holy Rosary of the Blessed Virgin Mary, that we may imitate what they contain and obtain what they promise, through the same Christ Our Lord. Amen.

Wednesday

THE GLORIOUS MYSTERIES

WEDNESDAY
The Glorious Mysteries

Make the
SIGN
of the
CROSS

Say the Apostles Creed:

I believe in God, the Father Almighty, Creator of
Heaven and earth; and in Jesus Christ, His only Son,
our Lord: Who was conceived by the Holy Spirit, born
of the Virgin Mary; suffered under Pontius Pilate, was
crucified, died and was buried. He descended into
hell; the third day He rose again from the dead; He
ascended into Heaven, is seated at the right hand of
God the Father Almighty; from thence He shall come
to judge the living and the dead. **I believe in the Holy
Spirit, the Holy Catholic Church, the communion of
Saints, the forgiveness of sins, the resurrection of the
body, and life everlasting. Amen.**

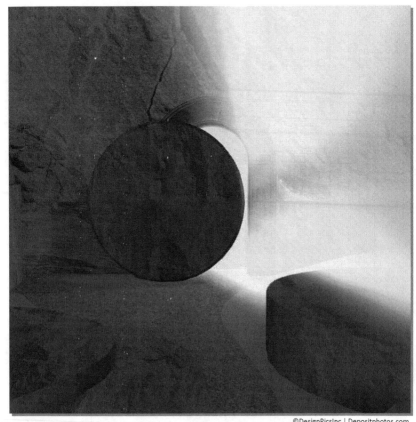

(Groups may wish to read the abridged, **bolded** sections of the Mystery only)

WEDNESDAY

1st Mystery

The Glorious Mysteries

The First Mystery: The Resurrection

Paraphrased from Luke 23:50-56, 24:1-44, John 20:1-29, Mark 16:1-13, Matthew 28:1-10 NAB

- A good man named Joseph asks Pilate for Jesus' body, so he can wrap it in linens and place it in the tomb.

- **The chief priests fear Jesus' body will be taken, so they place guards next to the tomb and a large stone blocking the entrance.**

- On the third day, the earth quakes and an angel rolls back the stone, sending the terrified guards running.

- **Mary Magdalene and some other women arrive at the tomb to anoint Jesus' body, but are frightened when they see that the tomb has been opened.**

- **An angel appears to them and says, " Do not be amazed! You are seeking Jesus of Nazareth, the crucified. He has been raised; he is not here."**

- **Jesus later appears to the disciples while they are behind locked doors, and shows them His hands and side to prove it's really Him.**

- **He then tells the overjoyed disciples, "Peace be with you. As the Father has sent me, so I send you."**

- Thank you, Jesus, for the gift of knowing the truth of Your Resurrection.

Spiritual Fruit : Faith

Oh my Jesus, forgive us our sins. Save us from the fires of hell. Lead all souls to Heaven, especially those in most need of Thy Mercy. Amen.

WEDNESDAY
The Glorious Mysteries

The Second Mystery: The Ascension

Portions Paraphrased from Luke 24:50-53 and Acts 1:1-12 NAB

- **Jesus appears to the disciples many times over the span of forty days after His Resurrection to prove He was truly alive.**

- Jesus tells the disciples that the Holy Spirit will soon be upon them.

- He tells them that they will be His witnesses and that they will preach His Gospel to the "ends of the earth."

- **Accompanied by the disciples and His Mother on Mt. Olivet, Jesus extends His pierced hands over them and gives them one last blessing.**

- **Jesus is then taken up to Heaven right in front of them, to take His place at the right hand of the Father.**

- **As the disciples continue to look up at the sky, two men dressed in white suddenly appear next to them.**

- **They said, "Why are you standing there looking at the sky? The Jesus who has been taken up from you into heaven will return in the same way as you have seen him going into heaven."**

- Mary, how overjoyed you must have been to see Your Son again after His Crucifixion! Thank you, God, for this gift to the Blessed Mother and to the whole world. We eagerly await His coming again.

Spiritual Fruit : Christian Hope

Oh my Jesus, forgive us our sins. Save us from the fires of hell. Lead all souls to Heaven, especially those in most need of Thy Mercy. Amen.

Pixabay.com

WEDNESDAY
The Glorious Mysteries

3rd Mystery

The Third Mystery: The Descent of the Holy Spirit

Portions paraphrased from Acts 2:1-47 NAB

- **The apostles and the Blessed Mother are praying in the room where Jesus held the Last Supper.**

- **Suddenly, a violent wind blows through the house, and what seems to be tongues of fire hover over each of the apostles' heads.**

- **Each of them is filled with the Holy Spirit, and they are suddenly able to speak in other languages.**

- A crowd that has gathered outside the house hears the apostles speaking in languages each of them understands.

- **Peter speaks up and addresses the crowd, quoting the prophets and explaining that Jesus fulfilled the prophesies; He really is the Messiah.**

- Many begin to believe Peter and feel remorse for the treatment of Christ.

- They ask Peter, what should they do? He tells them to repent and be baptized in the name of Jesus; they'll receive the gift of the Holy Spirit.

- **Peter baptizes three thousand people that day (Pentecost).**

- Father, thank You for continually sending Your Holy Spirit to guide and strengthen us. Help us to discern Your Spirit from false worldly promises.

Spiritual Fruit : Gifts of the Holy Spirit

Oh my Jesus, forgive us our sins. Save us from the fires of hell. Lead all souls to Heaven, especially those in most need of Thy Mercy. Amen.

Pixabay.com

WEDNESDAY
The Glorious Mysteries

4th Mystery

The Fourth Mystery: The Assumption

Portions paraphrased from 1 Corinthians 15:54 NAB, Pope Pius XII's Apostolic Constitution and the Apostles Creed

- **Mary goes to live with John the Apostle, just as Jesus alluded to as He was dying on the cross.**

- **Mary lives for many years after Her Son's death, and is a constant source of comfort, strength and support for the apostles.**

- **When Mary "dies", she is overcome by divine love and taken up, body and soul, into Heaven.**

- When the apostles arrive at Mary's tomb after her burial, all they find are fragrant lilies where her body would have lain.

- **Corruption of the body happens only to those born with original sin, and the Blessed Mother was born completely free of sin.**

- **We believe in the resurrection of the body, and life everlasting.**

- The bodies of all mankind will be united with the soul at the last judgment.

- When we pray to Mary, Our Blessed Mother lovingly picks us up and puts us on the path to Her Son. Thank you, Dear Mary, for showing us on the most direct path to Jesus.

Spiritual Fruit : To Jesus through Mary

Oh my Jesus, forgive us our sins. Save us from the fires of hell. Lead all souls to Heaven, especially those in most need of Thy Mercy. Amen.

Coronation of Mary by Catarino Veneziano 1360 (PD-1923 Wikimedia.org)

WEDNESDAY

The Glorious Mysteries

5th Mystery

The Fifth Mystery: The Coronation

Paraphrased from Revelation 12:1, Luke 1:48-49 NAB and Pope Pius XII's Ad Caeli Reginam

- As Mary enters Heaven, all the angels and saints greet her with great joy.

- Mary is crowned Queen of Heaven and earth by Her Son.

- "A great sign appeared in the sky, a woman clothed with the sun, with the moon under her feet , and on her head a crown of twelve stars."

- Mary shares in Jesus' glory in Heaven because she so fully shared in His suffering on earth.

- As Mary predicted to her cousin Elizabeth, "behold, from now on will all ages call me blessed. The Mighty One has done great things for me, and holy is his name."

- God gives Mary an exceptional role in the redemption of the entire human race.

- Mary intercedes for the salvation of our souls constantly.

- Not only is Mary a most powerful Queen, but she's also a most merciful and loving Mother.

- Thank you, God, for the wonderful gift of Our Mother and her unending love and mercy for us.

Spiritual Fruit : Grace of Final Perseverance

Oh my Jesus, forgive us our sins. Save us from the fires of hell. Lead all souls to Heaven, especially those in most need of Thy Mercy. Amen.

WEDNESDAY

The Glorious Mysteries

Hail, Holy Queen,

Mother of Mercy, our life, our sweetness, and our hope! To thee do we cry, poor, banished children of Eve; to thee do we send up our sighs, mourning and weeping in this valley of tears. Turn then, most gracious advocate, thine eyes of mercy toward us, and after this our exile, show unto us the blessed fruit of thy womb, Jesus. Oh clement, oh loving, oh sweet Virgin Mary! Pray for us, oh Holy Mother of God, that we may be made worthy of the promises of Christ. Amen.

Let us pray, oh God, Whose only begotten Son, by His life, death, and resurrection, has purchased for us the rewards of eternal life, grant, we beseech Thee, that by meditating upon these mysteries of the Most Holy Rosary of the Blessed Virgin Mary, that we may imitate what they contain and obtain what they promise, through the same Christ Our Lord. Amen.

Thursday

THE LUMINOUS MYSTERIES

©Forestpath | Dreamstime.com

THURSDAY
The Luminous Mysteries

Say the **Apostles Creed**.

I believe in God, the Father Almighty, Creator of Heaven and earth; and in Jesus Christ, His only Son, our Lord: Who was conceived by the Holy Spirit, born of the Virgin Mary; suffered under Pontius Pilate, was crucified, died and was buried. He descended into hell; the third day He rose again from the dead; He ascended into Heaven, is seated at the right hand of God the Father Almighty; from thence He shall come to judge the living and the dead. **I believe in the Holy Spirit, the Holy Catholic Church, the communion of Saints, the forgiveness of sins, the resurrection of the body, and life everlasting. Amen.**

THURSDAY

1st Mystery

The Luminous Mysteries

The First Mystery: The Baptism of the Lord

Portions paraphrased from Mark 1:4-8 and Matthew 3:13-17 NAB

- John the Baptist was baptizing people from Jerusalem and the Judean countryside in the Jordan River.

- John tells them, "I have baptized you with water; he will baptize you with the holy Spirit. "

- Jesus travels from Galilee to be baptized by John.

- **John tells Jesus he's not worthy to baptize Him, but Jesus tells John that by doing so he would "fulfill all righteousness."**

- **John baptizes Jesus in the Jordan, and baptism becomes a sacrament.**

- **As Jesus comes up out of the water, the Holy Spirit comes down on Him "like a dove".**

- **A voice from Heaven says, "You are my beloved Son; with you I am well pleased."**

- **Here the divine Trinity of the Father, Son and Holy Spirit are all present at the same time.**

- Lord, You bless us with Your sacraments continually, from the time we are born to the time we die. Thank You for the freedom from original sin that we receive during the sacrament of baptism.

Spiritual Fruit : Gratitude for the Gift of Faith

Oh my Jesus, forgive us our sins. Save us from the fires of hell. Lead all souls to Heaven, especially those in most need of Thy Mercy. Amen.

Pixabay.com

THURSDAY

The Luminous Mysteries

2nd Mystery

The Second Mystery: The Wedding of Cana

Portions paraphrased from John 2:1-11 NAB

- Jesus, His Mother and His disciples attend a wedding in Cana.

- Mary tells Her Son the wedding hosts have run out of wine.

- Jesus asks His Mother what she wants Him to do; "My hour has not yet come."

- Mary tells the servants to do whatever Jesus tells them to do.

- Jesus tell the servants to fill some jars with water, and draw some out and take it to the headwaiter.

- Not realizing Jesus had turned the water into wine, the headwaiter calls over the groom.

- "Everyone serves good wine first, and then when people have drunk freely, an inferior one; but you have kept the good wine until now."

- At Mary's request, Jesus worked His first miracle, and His disciples began to believe in Him.

- Jesus is so loyal to His Mother that He never rejects her requests. Thank you, Dear Mary, for your constant intercession on our behalf, and for taking every one of our intentions to Your Son.

Spiritual Fruit : Fidelity

Oh my Jesus, forgive us our sins. Save us from the fires of hell. Lead all souls to Heaven, especially those in most need of Thy Mercy. Amen.

Christ and Child by Carl Heinrich Bloch, 1873 (PD-1923 Wikimedia.org)

THURSDAY

3rd Mystery

The Luminous Mysteries

The Third Mystery: The Proclamation of the Kingdom

Portions paraphrased from Mark 1:15, John 3:5 and Matthew 18:4 NAB

- **John the Baptist is put in prison, and Jesus goes into Galilee to proclaim the gospel of God.**

- **Jesus says, "This is the time of fulfillment. The kingdom of God is at hand. Repent, and believe in the gospel."**

- Jesus travels and teaches many people about the kingdom of God before his crucifixion.

- **Jesus says to the Jewish leader, Nicodemus: "Amen, amen, I say to you, no one can enter the kingdom of God without being born of water and spirit."**

- **When the disciples ask Jesus who is the greatest in Heaven, He tells them: "Whoever humbles himself like this little child is the greatest in the kingdom of heaven."**

- **Pharisees ask the disciples why Jesus is eating with tax collectors and sinners, and Jesus says, "Those who are well do not need a physician, but the sick do. I did not come to call the righteous, but sinners."**

- Lord, help me develop the traits that are truly important to You; love of You, love of neighbor and enemy, humility, kindness and tolerance.

Spiritual Fruit : Desire for Holiness

Oh my Jesus, forgive us our sins. Save us from the fires of hell. Lead all souls to Heaven, especially those in most need of Thy Mercy. Amen.

Church of the Most Holy Rosary, Tullow, Ireland (Photograph by Andreas F. Borchart CC 3.0 Germany Wikimedia.org)

THURSDAY
The Luminous Mysteries

The Fourth Mystery: The Transfiguration

Portions paraphrased from Matthew 17:1-13 and Luke 9:28-36 NAB

- **Jesus takes Peter, James and John up a high mountain to pray.**

- **While Jesus is praying, His face and clothes became dazzling white.**

- **Moses and Elijah, both prophets from the Old Testament, suddenly appear and begin speaking with Jesus.**

- Peter, confused by what he's seeing, offers to make three tents; one for Jesus, one for Moses and one for Elijah.

- **A bright cloud appears over them and a voice says, "This is my beloved Son, with whom I am well pleased; listen to him."**

- The disciples, afraid, lie down face-first on the ground.

- Jesus tells them, "Rise, and do not be afraid." When they look up, Elijah and Moses are gone.

- **Jesus tells the disciples not to tell anyone what they have seen until "the Son of Man has been raised from the dead."**

- Jesus was transfigured before the disciples so they could withstand the tragedy of His coming Passion. Thank you, Lord, for giving us what we need to endure each of our life's trials.

Spiritual Fruit : Spiritual Courage

Oh my Jesus, forgive us our sins. Save us from the fires of hell. Lead all souls to Heaven, especially those in most need of Thy Mercy. Amen.

THURSDAY
The Luminous Mysteries

5th
Mystery

The Fifth Mystery: The Institution of the Eucharist

Portions paraphrased from Luke 22:7-20 and John 6:48-56 NAB

- While preaching in Capernaum, Jesus says, "I am the living bread that came down from heaven; whoever eats this bread will live forever; and the bread that I will give is my flesh for the life of the world."

- **On the Passover before His Passion, Jesus tells Peter and John to go into the city and find a man carrying a jug of water.**

- **They were to follow the man into a house where they would be led to a room where Jesus and the disciples would eat their Passover meal.**

- Peter and John follow Jesus' instructions, and find everything exactly as He had said. They prepare the meal.

- **During the meal, Jesus says to the disciples, "I have eagerly desired to eat this Passover with you before I suffer…"**

- **He took the bread, blessed it, broke it and gave it to them and said "This is my body, which will be given for you; do this in memory of me."**

- **After they ate the bread, Jesus took the wine and said, "This cup is the new covenant in my blood, which will be shed for you."**

- God physically presents Himself during every Mass in the Eucharist. Thank you, Dear Lord, for Your gift of this personal communion with You.

Spiritual Fruit : Love of Our Eucharistic Lord

Oh my Jesus, forgive us our sins. Save us from the fires of hell. Lead all souls to Heaven, especially those in most need of Thy Mercy. Amen.

89

THURSDAY
The Luminous Mysteries

Hail, Holy Queen,

Mother of Mercy, our life, our sweetness, and our hope! To thee do we cry, poor, banished children of Eve; to thee do we send up our sighs, mourning and weeping in this valley of tears. Turn then, most gracious advocate, thine eyes of mercy toward us, and after this our exile, show unto us the blessed fruit of thy womb, Jesus. Oh clement, oh loving, oh sweet Virgin Mary! Pray for us, oh Holy Mother of God, that we may be made worthy of the promises of Christ. Amen.

Let us pray, oh God, Whose only begotten Son, by His life, death, and resurrection, has purchased for us the rewards of eternal life, grant, we beseech Thee, that by meditating upon these mysteries of the Most Holy Rosary of the Blessed Virgin Mary, that we may imitate what they contain and obtain what they promise, through the same Christ Our Lord. Amen.

Friday

THE SORROWFUL MYSTERIES

The Pieta by Michelangelo, St. Peter's Basilica, Vatican City (Photograph by Jebulon CC 1.0 PD Wikimedia.org)

FRIDAY

The Sorrowful Mysteries

Make the
SIGN
of the
CROSS

Say the **Apostles Creed:**

I believe in God, the Father Almighty, Creator of Heaven and earth; and in Jesus Christ, His only Son, our Lord: Who was conceived by the Holy Spirit, born of the Virgin Mary; suffered under Pontius Pilate, was crucified, died and was buried. He descended into hell; the third day He rose again from the dead; He ascended into Heaven, is seated at the right hand of God the Father Almighty; from thence He shall come to judge the living and the dead. **I believe in the Holy Spirit, the Holy Catholic Church, the communion of Saints, the forgiveness of sins, the resurrection of the body, and life everlasting. Amen.**

Christ on the Mount of Olives by Gyula Benczur, 1919 (PD-1923 Wikimedia.org)

(Groups may wish to read the abridged, bolded sections of the Mystery only)

FRIDAY

1st Mystery

The Sorrowful Mysteries

The First Mystery: The Agony in the Garden

Portions paraphrased from Luke 22:39-46 and Matthew 26:36-46 NAB

- **Jesus and His disciples went to a place called Gethsemane to pray.**

- **Jesus tells Peter, James and John that His soul is, "overwhelmed with sorrow to the point of death."**

- **He walks a short distance away from them and prays, "Father, if you are willing, take this cup away from me; still, not my will but yours be done."**

- **Here Jesus foresees the sins of all mankind, and is so overcome with anguish that His sweat becomes drops of blood.**

- An angel appears to Him to strengthen Him.

- **He returns to the sleeping disciples and says to Peter, "So you could not keep watch with me for one hour? Watch and pray that you may not undergo the test."**

- Even though the disciples disappointed Jesus in His simple request, He forgave them and loved them fully.

- In that same way, Jesus forgives me of my sins and loves me. How can I be more like Christ in my forgiveness and love of others?

Spiritual Fruit : God's Will Be Done

Oh my Jesus, forgive us our sins. Save us from the fires of hell. Lead all souls to Heaven, especially those in most need of Thy Mercy. Amen.

FRIDAY

The Sorrowful Mysteries

The Second Mystery: The Scourging at the Pillar

Portions paraphrased from Mark 15:1-15, John 19:1-4 and Isaiah 53:5 NAB

- Jesus is taken to the Jewish High Priest, where He is insulted and falsely accused.

- The Jewish leaders take Jesus to Pilate, since only he can order the death penalty.

- Pilate can "find no guilt in him", but to appease the Jews, he orders that Jesus be scourged.

- The Romans tie Jesus to a pillar and fiercely scourge Him with a short, whip-like weapon that has sharp bones or iron balls on the end of it.

- This painful scourging fulfills Isaiah's prophesy from the Old Testament, that Jesus would be "pierced for our sins" and "crushed for our iniquity".

- It's believed the Blessed Mother, Mary Magdalene and other apostles witnessed the scourging of Jesus.

- Jesus suffered so intensely to make up for our sins. Heavenly Father, for the sake of His sorrowful passion, have mercy on us and on the whole world.

Spiritual Fruit : Mortification of the Senses

Oh my Jesus, forgive us our sins. Save us from the fires of hell. Lead all souls to Heaven, especially those in most need of Thy Mercy. Amen.

FRIDAY

The Sorrowful Mysteries

The Third Mystery: The Crowning with Thorns

Portions paraphrased from Matthew 27:11-29, John 18:33-36 and 19:1-5 NAB

- **Pilate asks, "Are you the King of the Jews?" Jesus responds, "My kingdom does not belong to this world."**

- The Roman soldiers take Jesus into the praetorium (or "common hall") and gather all around Him.

- **The soldiers strip Jesus and put an old purple cloak on Him.**

- **They twist together a crown of thorns and push it into Jesus' head.**

- They put a staff in His right hand, spit on Him and mock Him for saying He is a king.

- **"Hail, king of the Jews!" they shout, and they take the staff from His hand and hit Him on the head with it several times.**

- They then strip the cloak off Jesus' bloodied back and shoulders and put His original clothes back on.

- **The soldiers then lead Jesus away to be crucified.**

- Lord, help me to recognize the dignity You instilled in every one of Your children. Help me show respect and kindness to others, even if I don't agree with them.

Spiritual Fruit : Reign of Christ in Our Hearts

Oh my Jesus, forgive us our sins. Save us from the fires of hell. Lead all souls to Heaven, especially those in most need of Thy Mercy. Amen.

Pixabay.com

FRIDAY
The Sorrowful Mysteries

4th Mystery

The Fourth Mystery: The Carrying of the Cross

Paraphrased from Matthew 27:32-33, John 19:17, Luke 23:26-31 NAB, Stations of the Cross

- **Jesus is forced to carry His own cross to the place where He will be crucified, called Golgotha, or "Place of the Skull".**

- The cross is heavy, and Jesus is weakened from the scourging and lack of food, water and sleep.

- **Jesus falls under the weight of the cross three times.**

- **He sees His Mother in the crowd, and they exchange a poignant glance.**

- **Seeing that He's become too weak to continue on His own, the soldiers order Simon of Cyrene to help Jesus carry His cross.**

- A woman in the crowd named Veronica has deep pity for Jesus as He passes by, and she wipes His face with her veil.

- A miraculous impression of Jesus' face is left on the cloth.

- **Jesus says to the crying women who were following Him, "...do not weep for me; weep instead for yourselves and for your children."**

- Mary, how horrible it must have been to see your Son in this agony. Thank you for lovingly and empathetically holding us close during our most difficult times.

Spiritual Fruit : Patient Bearing of Trials

Oh my Jesus, forgive us our sins. Save us from the fires of hell. Lead all souls to Heaven, especially those in most need of Thy Mercy. Amen.

FRIDAY

The Sorrowful Mysteries

The Fifth Mystery: The Crucifixion

Portions paraphrased from Mark 15:21-41 and Luke 23:32-46 NAB

- **The soldiers bind and then nail Jesus' hands and feet to the cross.**

- **Jesus prays as He is being crucified, "Father, forgive them, they know not what they do."**

- One of the two criminals being crucified next to Jesus challenges Him, telling Jesus to save Himself and them if He's really the One.

- The other criminal humbly asks Jesus to remember him when He comes into His kingdom, and Jesus replies, "Amen, I say to you, today you will be with me in Paradise."

- **Around 3PM, Jesus cries out, "My God, my God, why have you forsaken me?"**

- **And then, in a loud voice, Jesus says, "Father, into your hands I commend my spirit," and He breathed His last breath and died.**

- **Jesus is taken down off the cross and laid in the arms of His Mother.**

- Mary, how painful it must have been to hold Your Son in your arms after He died. Thank you for holding me in those same loving arms. Please help me to console others by sharing your love.

Spiritual Fruit : Pardoning of Injuries

Oh my Jesus, forgive us our sins. Save us from the fires of hell. Lead all souls to Heaven, especially those in most need of Thy Mercy. Amen.

FRIDAY

The Sorrowful Mysteries

Hail, Holy Queen,

Mother of Mercy, our life, our sweetness, and our hope! To thee do we cry, poor, banished children of Eve; to thee do we send up our sighs, mourning and weeping in this valley of tears. Turn then, most gracious advocate, thine eyes of mercy toward us, and after this our exile, show unto us the blessed fruit of thy womb, Jesus. Oh clement, oh loving, oh sweet Virgin Mary! Pray for us, oh Holy Mother of God, that we may be made worthy of the promises of Christ. Amen.

Let us pray, oh God, Whose only begotten Son, by His life, death, and resurrection, has purchased for us the rewards of eternal life, grant, we beseech Thee, that by meditating upon these mysteries of the Most Holy Rosary of the Blessed Virgin Mary, that we may imitate what they contain and obtain what they promise, through the same Christ Our Lord. Amen.

Saturday

THE JOYFUL MYSTERIES

Pixabay.com

SATURDAY

The Joyful Mysteries

Make the **SIGN** of the **CROSS**

Say the **Apostles Creed**:

I believe in God, the Father Almighty, Creator of Heaven and earth; and in Jesus Christ, His only Son, our Lord: Who was conceived by the Holy Spirit, born of the Virgin Mary; suffered under Pontius Pilate, was crucified, died and was buried. He descended into hell; the third day He rose again from the dead; He ascended into Heaven, is seated at the right hand of God the Father Almighty; from thence He shall come to judge the living and the dead. **I believe in the Holy Spirit, the Holy Catholic Church, the communion of Saints, the forgiveness of sins, the resurrection of the body, and life everlasting. Amen.**

(Groups may wish to read the abridged, bolded sections of the Mystery only)

SATURDAY

The Joyful Mysteries

The First Mystery: The Annunciation

Portions paraphrased from Luke 1: 26-38 NAB

- God prepared Mary from her conception to be the Mother of Jesus, free from original sin.

- **The Angel Gabriel appears to Mary and greets her.**

- **Mary is frightened and confused.**

- Gabriel assures her: "Do not be afraid, Mary, for you have found favor with God."

- He says: **"Behold, you will conceive in your womb and bear a son, and you shall name him Jesus."**

- **Mary is worried because she's pledged to be married to Joseph, and has made a vow of virginity.**

- During this time in history, a woman could be stoned to death for becoming pregnant out of wedlock.

- **Mary considers all of this and bravely answers: "Behold, I am the handmaid of the Lord. May it be it done unto me according to your word."**

- Lord, am I working towards what I want, or what You want?

Spiritual Fruit : Humility

SATURDAY
The Joyful Mysteries

The Second Mystery: The Visitation

Portions paraphrased from Luke 1:39-45 NAB

- Mary's cousin, Elizabeth, had become pregnant, despite her age and many years of infertility.

- When Mary hears the news, she plans to visit Elizabeth, even though they live 80 miles apart and Mary is newly pregnant herself.

- The journey is long and difficult, but Mary is joyful because she knows she's carrying the Son of God.

- When Mary arrives, Elizabeth's baby jumps in her womb at the sound of Mary's voice.

- Elizabeth says, "And how does this happen to me, that the mother of my Lord should come to me?"

- Mary replies, "My soul proclaims the greatness of the Lord and my spirit rejoices in God my savior."

- Mary stays with Elizabeth and helps her for the next three months until the birth of John the Baptist.

- Am I available when someone needs me, or only when it's convenient for me? Lord, help me to discern when someone truly needs my help, and please give me the strength to assist them in their need.

Spiritual Fruit : Love of Neighbor

SATURDAY

3rd Mystery

The Joyful Mysteries

The Third Mystery: The Nativity

Portions paraphrased from Luke 2:1-20 NAB

- Caesar Augustus required that everyone in the Roman domain register for the census in their native town.

- Joseph's family was from Bethlehem, so he and Mary travel from Nazareth to Bethlehem to register.

- **When they arrive in Bethlehem, Mary goes into labor, and she and Joseph try to find a room at the inn.**

- **There's no room for them there, so Mary gives birth to Her Son in a cave, wraps Him in cloths, and lays Him in a manger.**

- **Jesus is born into poverty to teach detachment from earthly things.**

- **Mary, still a Virgin, is utterly joyful as she cradles Her Son.**

- **An angel appears to shepherds nearby and says, "...today in the city of David a Savior has been born for you who is Messiah and Lord."**

- Mary, help me to recognize which of my earthly/ material things I can share with others, so that we both might benefit spiritually from me sharing with them.

Spiritual Fruit : Poverty of Spirit

Oh my Jesus, forgive us our sins. Save us from the fires of hell. Lead all souls to Heaven, especially those in most need of Thy Mercy. Amen.

SATURDAY

4th Mystery

The Joyful Mysteries

The Fourth Mystery: The Presentation

Portions paraphrased from Luke 2:22-40 NAB

- The Law of Moses required that every family consecrate (or, "dedicate") their firstborn son to the Lord.

- **Mary and Joseph bring Jesus to the temple for His consecration.**

- Simeon was a "righteous and devout" man who had been told by the Holy Spirit that he would see the Messiah before he died.

- **When the Holy Family enters the temple, Simeon immediately recognizes Jesus.**

- Simeon takes Jesus into his arms and says, "Now, Master, you may let your servant go in peace, according to your word, for mine eyes have seen your salvation..."

- **Mary and Joseph are amazed at what Simeon says about Jesus.**

- **Simeon tells Mary, "Behold, this child is destined for the fall and rise of many in Israel, and to be a sign that will be contradicted (and you yourself a sword will pierce)..."**

- Mary, please help me to have the kind of faith and trust you and Joseph had, especially as you began to see how extraordinary God's plan was for your family.

Spiritual Fruit : Purity of Mind and Body

Finding in the Temple fresco, Kirchenstrasse, Carinthia, Austria (Photo by Johann Jaritz 2011 CCO 3.0 Unported Wikimedia.org)

SATURDAY

5th Mystery

The Joyful Mysteries

The Fifth Mystery: The Finding of Jesus in the Temple

Portions paraphrased from Luke 2:41-52 NAB

- **When Jesus is twelve years old, Mary and Joseph take Him with them to the festival of the Passover.**

- **When the festival is over, Mary and Joseph set off for home, unknowingly without Jesus.**

- Once Mary and Joseph realize Jesus is missing, they start frantically searching for Him.

- **After three days of searching, they find Jesus in the temple in Jerusalem, talking with the teachers and doctors.**

- Everyone listening to Jesus is amazed by His knowledge and perspective.

- **When Mary tells Jesus she and Joseph were anxiously looking for Him, Jesus says, "Why were you looking for Me? Did you not know that I must be in my Father's house?"**

- **Jesus goes home with Mary and Joseph and is obedient to them.**

- In what situations do I tend to worry unnecessarily or try to take control? Mary, help me to remember that God is in control, and to trust Him with my whole heart under all circumstances.

Spiritual Fruit : Obedience

SATURDAY

The Joyful Mysteries

Hail, Holy Queen,

Mother of Mercy, our life, our sweetness, and our hope! To thee do we cry, poor, banished children of Eve; to thee do we send up our sighs, mourning and weeping in this valley of tears. Turn then, most gracious advocate, thine eyes of mercy toward us, and after this our exile, show unto us the blessed fruit of thy womb, Jesus. Oh clement, oh loving, oh sweet Virgin Mary! Pray for us, oh Holy Mother of God, that we may be made worthy of the promises of Christ. Amen.

Let us pray, oh God, Whose only begotten Son, by His life, death, and resurrection, has purchased for us the rewards of eternal life, grant, we beseech Thee, that by meditating upon these mysteries of the Most Holy Rosary of the Blessed Virgin Mary, that we may imitate what they contain and obtain what they promise, through the same Christ Our Lord. Amen.

Sunday

THE GLORIOUS MYSTERIES

Pixabay.com

SUNDAY

The Glorious Mysteries

Make the
SIGN
of the
CROSS

Say the **Apostles Creed**:

I believe in God, the Father Almighty, Creator of Heaven and earth; and in Jesus Christ, His only Son, our Lord: Who was conceived by the Holy Spirit, born of the Virgin Mary; suffered under Pontius Pilate, was crucified, died and was buried. He descended into hell; the third day He rose again from the dead; He ascended into Heaven, is seated at the right hand of God the Father Almighty; from thence He shall come to judge the living and the dead. **I believe in the Holy Spirit, the Holy Catholic Church, the communion of Saints, the forgiveness of sins, the resurrection of the body, and life everlasting. Amen.**

Pixabay.com

SUNDAY

The Glorious Mysteries

1st Mystery

The First Mystery: The Resurrection

Paraphrased from Luke 23:50-56, 24:1-44, John 20:1-29, Mark 16:1-13, Matthew 28:1-10 NAB

- A good man named Joseph asks Pilate for Jesus' body, so he can wrap it in linens and place it in the tomb.

- **The chief priests fear Jesus' body will be taken, so they place guards next to the tomb and a large stone blocking the entrance.**

- On the third day, the earth quakes and an angel rolls back the stone, sending the terrified guards running.

- **Mary Magdalene and some other women arrive at the tomb to anoint Jesus' body, but are frightened when they see that the tomb has been opened.**

- **An angel appears to them and says, " Do not be amazed! You are seeking Jesus of Nazareth, the crucified. He has been raised; he is not here."**

- **Jesus later appears to the disciples while they are behind locked doors, and shows them His hands and side to prove it's really Him.**

- **He then tells the overjoyed disciples, "Peace be with you. As the Father has sent me, so I send you."**

- Dear Mary, help me discern how to share this Good News with others.

Spiritual Fruit : Faith

Oh my Jesus, forgive us our sins. Save us from the fires of hell. Lead all souls to Heaven, especially those in most need of Thy Mercy. Amen.

Christ the Redeemer, Rio de Janeiro | Pixabay.com

SUNDAY

2nd Mystery

The Glorious Mysteries

The Second Mystery: The Ascension

Portions paraphrased from Luke 24:50-53 and Acts 1:1-12 NAB

- **Jesus appears to the disciples many times over the span of forty days after His Resurrection to prove He was truly alive.**

- Jesus tells the disciples that the Holy Spirit will soon be upon them.

- He tells them that they will be His witnesses and that they will preach His Gospel to the "ends of the earth."

- **Accompanied by the disciples and His Mother on Mt. Olivet, Jesus extends His pierced hands over them and gives them one last blessing.**

- **Jesus is then taken up to Heaven right in front of them, to take His place at the right hand of the Father.**

- **As the disciples continue to look up at the sky, two men dressed in white suddenly appear next to them.**

- **They said, "Why are you standing there looking at the sky? The Jesus who has been taken up from you into heaven will return in the same way as you have seen him going into heaven."**

- Thank you, God , for not only sacrificing Your Son for the sins of the world, but also for this evidence of His Resurrection.

Spiritual Fruit : Christian Hope

Oh my Jesus, forgive us our sins. Save us from the fires of hell. Lead all souls to Heaven, especially those in most need of Thy Mercy. Amen.

From the Dominican Order church in the town of Friesach, Carinthia, Austria (CCO 1.0 Public Domain Wikimedia.org)

SUNDAY

The Glorious Mysteries

The Third Mystery: The Descent of the Holy Spirit

Portions paraphrased from Acts 2:1-47 NAB

- **The apostles and the Blessed Mother are praying in the room where Jesus held the Last Supper.**

- **Suddenly, a violent wind blows through the house, and what seems to be tongues of fire hover over each of the apostles' heads.**

- **Each of them is filled with the Holy Spirit, and they are suddenly able to speak in other languages.**

- A crowd that has gathered outside the house hears the apostles speaking in languages each of them understands.

- **Peter speaks up and addresses the crowd, quoting the prophets and explaining that Jesus fulfilled the prophesies; He really is the Messiah.**

- Many begin to believe Peter and feel remorse for the treatment of Christ.

- They ask Peter, what should they do? He tells them to repent and be baptized in the name of Jesus; they'll receive the gift of the Holy Spirit.

- **Peter baptizes three thousand people that day (Pentecost).**

- Mary, help me to recognize and nurture the gifts of the Holy Spirit in me and those around me, so that we may use those gifts to glorify God.

Spiritual Fruit : Gifts of the Holy Spirit

Oh my Jesus, forgive us our sins. Save us from the fires of hell. Lead all souls to Heaven, especially those in most need of Thy Mercy. Amen.

Tomb of the Virgin Mary, Jerusalem (Photo by WomEOS 2009 CCO 2.0 Generic Wikimedia.org)

SUNDAY

The Glorious Mysteries

The Fourth Mystery: The Assumption

Portions paraphrased from 1 Corinthians 15:54, Pope Pius XII's Apostolic Constitution and the Apostles Creed

- **Mary goes to live with John the Apostle, just as Jesus alluded to as He was dying on the cross.**

- **Mary lives for many years after Her Son's death, and is a constant source of comfort, strength and support for the apostles.**

- **When Mary "dies", she is overcome by divine love and taken up, body and soul, into Heaven.**

- When the apostles arrive at Mary's tomb after her burial, all they find are fragrant lilies where her body would have lain.

- **Corruption of the body happens only to those born with original sin, and the Blessed Mother was born completely free of sin.**

- **We believe in the resurrection of the body, and life everlasting.**

- The bodies of all mankind will be united with the soul at the last judgment.

- Mary, your care and support of us is such a great gift. Thank you for your motherly involvement in our lives, and for lovingly taking every one of our intentions directly to Your Son.

Spiritual Fruit : To Jesus through Mary

Oh my Jesus, forgive us our sins. Save us from the fires of hell. Lead all souls to Heaven, especially those in most need of Thy Mercy. Amen.

Pixabay.com

SUNDAY
The Glorious Mysteries

The Fifth Mystery: The Coronation

Paraphrased from Revelation 12:1, Luke 1:48-49 NAB and Pope Pius XII's Ad Caeli Reginam

- As Mary enters Heaven, the angels and saints greet her with great joy.

- Mary is crowned Queen of Heaven and earth by Her Son.

- "A great sign appeared in the sky, a woman clothed with the sun, with the moon under her feet , and on her head a crown of twelve stars."

- Mary shares in Jesus' glory in Heaven because she so fully shared in His suffering on earth.

- As Mary predicted to her cousin Elizabeth, "behold, from now on will all ages call me blessed. The Mighty One has done great things fore me, and holy is his name."

- God gives Mary an exceptional role in the redemption of the entire human race.

- Mary intercedes for the salvation of our souls constantly.

- Not only is Mary a most powerful Queen, but she's also a most merciful and loving Mother.

- Mary is always ready and waiting to pray for us—for every person, under any circumstance—all we have to do is ask her.

Spiritual Fruit : Grace of Final Perseverance

Oh my Jesus, forgive us our sins. Save us from the fires of hell. Lead all souls to Heaven, especially those in most need of Thy Mercy. Amen.

SUNDAY

The Glorious Mysteries

Hail, Holy Queen,

Mother of Mercy, our life, our sweetness, and our hope! To thee do we cry, poor, banished children of Eve; to thee do we send up our sighs, mourning and weeping in this valley of tears. Turn then, most gracious advocate, thine eyes of mercy toward us, and after this our exile, show unto us the blessed fruit of thy womb, Jesus. Oh clement, oh loving, oh sweet Virgin Mary! Pray for us, oh Holy Mother of God, that we may be made worthy of the promises of Christ. Amen.

Let us pray, oh God, Whose only begotten Son, by His life, death, and resurrection, has purchased for us the rewards of eternal life, grant, we beseech Thee, that by meditating upon these mysteries of the Most Holy Rosary of the Blessed Virgin Mary, that we may imitate what they contain and obtain what they promise, through the same Christ Our Lord. Amen.

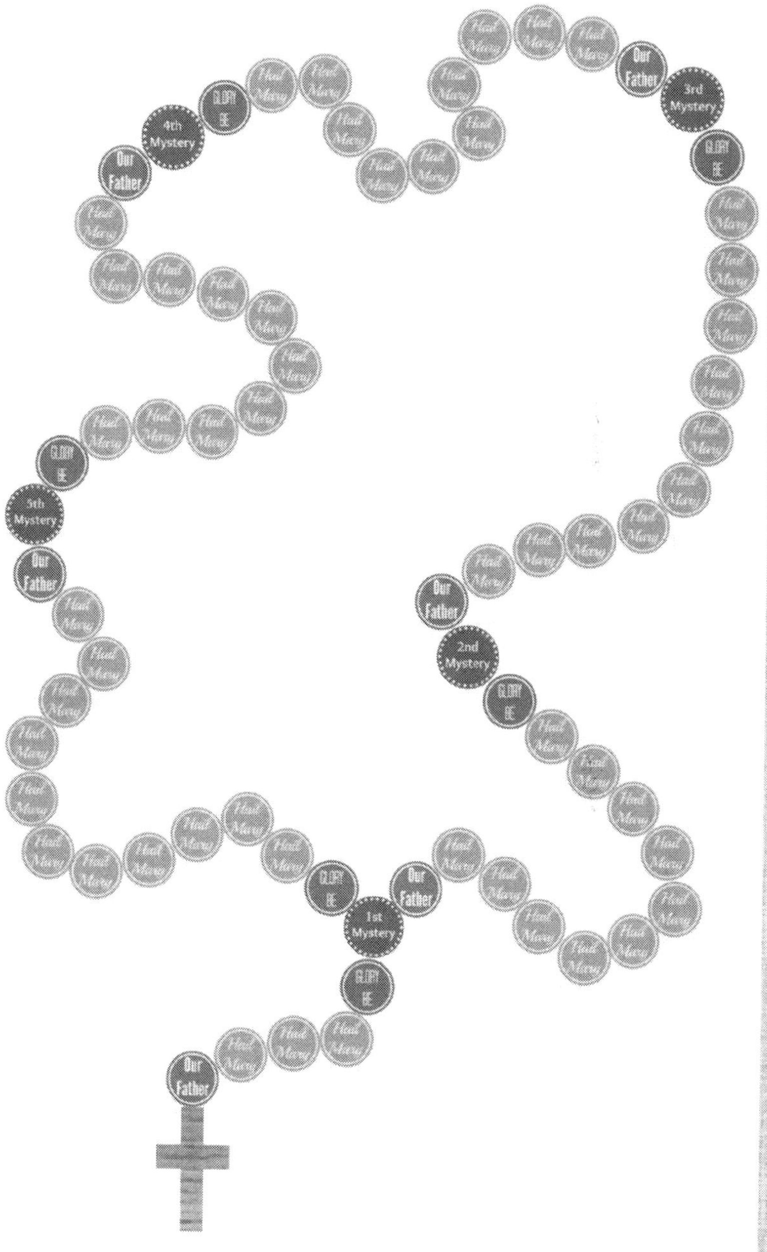
Our Father
Hail Mary
GLORY BE
1st Mystery
2nd Mystery
3rd Mystery
4th Mystery
5th Mystery

Prayer Log / Grace Notes

Bibliography/ Biblical References

(All Biblical References from the New American Bible, Revised Edition ©2010, 1991, 1986, 1970)

- Introduction- "devoted himself to Mary" St. Louis de Montfort (originally written in 1712, republished 2010). *True Devotion to Mary.* TAN Books, p.4.
- Introduction- "revealed to St. Dominic in an apparition" St. Lous de Montfort (Originally written in 1716, republished 1993). *The Secret of the Rosary.* TAN Books, pp.14-16.
- Introduction- "prayer being scientifically proven to reduce anxiety and depression as well as improve optimism": Boelens P.A., Reeves R.R., Replogle W.H., Koenig H.G. (2009) A randomized trial of the effect of prayer on depression and anxiety. *International Journal of Psychiatry in Medicine*; 39(4): 377-92.
- Mary's 15 Promises – This version appears on EWTN.com and Rosary-Center.org.
- Monday/ Sunday Mysteries– Portions paraphrased from Luke 1:26-38, 1:39-45, 2:1-20, 2:22-40 and 2:41-52.
- Tuesday/ Friday Mysteries– Portions paraphrased from Luke 22:39-46 and 23:26-46, Matthew 26:36-46, 27:11-29 and 27:32-33, Mark 15:15, Isaiah 53:5, John 18:33-36, 19:1, 19:5 and 19:17 and the Stations of the Cross.
- Tuesday/ Friday description of scourging at the pillar – Edwards, William D, MD, Gabel, Wesley J., Mdiv, Hosmer, Floyd E., MS, AMI, "The Physical Death of Jesus Christ". CatholicCulture.org. Trinity Communications, 1986. Accessed 10/15.
- Tuesday / Friday "It is believed the Blessed Mother, Mary Magdalene and other apostles witnessed the scourging of Jesus" from *The Dolorous Passion of Our Lord Jesus Christ*, written from the meditations of Anne Catherine Emmerich, an Augustian nun recognized as the recipient of mystic visions.
- Wednesday/ Sunday Mysteries- Portions paraphrased from Luke 23:50-56 and 24:50-53, John 20:1-29, Mark 16:1-13, Matthew 28:1-10, Acts 1:1-12, Acts 2:1-47, 1 Corinthians 15:54, Pope Pius XII's Apostolic Constitution, the Apostles Creed and Pope Pius XII's Ad Caeli Reginam.

- Thursday Mysteries- Portions Paraphrased from Mark 1:4-8 and 1:15, Matthew 3:13-17, 17:1-13 and 18:4, John 2:1-11, 3:5 and 6:48-56 and Luke 9:28-36 and 22:7-20.
- Many of the summaries of the 20 Mysteries were based on those provided on the website Rosary-Center.org, operated by the Dominican Fathers in Portland (with permission).

52704104R00083

Made in the USA
Charleston, SC
21 February 2016